Awesome Art Projects That Spark Super Writing

25 Motivating Art Projects With Mini-Lessons That Help Students Build Skills in Narrative, Expository, Persuasive, and Descriptive Writing

JAN WIEZOREK

New York • Toronto • London • Auckland • Sydney
Mexico City • New Delhi • Hong Kong • Buenos Aires

Teaching *Resources*

This book is dedicated to the sixth-, seventh-, and eighth-grade writers and artists
I have had the honor of teaching at St. Matthias School in Chicago.
Their rich artistic imagination and creativity are here for all to see.

I give thanks to God who led me to the ministry of teaching.

My fellow teachers and administrators deserve great thanks,
especially Sandria Morten, Sheila Klich, Mike Battle, and Margie Rosmonowski.

I remember fondly my mentor, Frank E. Brandt, who taught me to enjoy life through the arts.

Thank you, Paul Larson, for being a lifesaver.

Also, I thank editor Mela Ottaiano for sharing her insights.

Finally, the memory of my parents, Virginia and E. J. Wiezorek, inspires me even now.

Edited by Mela Ottaiano
Cover designed by Maria Lilja
Interior designed by Solas

ISBN: 978-0-545-30555-6
Copyright © 2011 by Jan Wiezorek
All rights reserved. Published by Scholastic Inc. Printed in the U.S.A.

4 5 6 7 8 9 10   40   17 16 15 14 13

Contents

Introduction

Every day, students struggle with their ideas and ability to put their thoughts on paper. Add to that task the complexity of using proper spelling, grammar, and punctuation—not to mention employing powerful verbs and interesting word choices—and it is easy to see that written communication challenges nearly every student. This collection of motivating art projects features 25 surefire ways to erase writer's block. The mini-lessons and creativity-boosting activities in *Awesome Art Projects That Spark Super Writing* help students as they learn to craft a coherent story, develop and support a main idea, describe a scene using precise words, and build a persuasive argument—learning to love writing along the way.

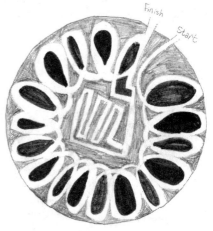

by Jerica C., eighth grade

Engaging students through the arts is an important first step. Typically, students express themselves through art with little struggle. So why not make "language arts" live up to its name? Let it begin with the visual arts and continue with expressive language compositions. Let it be a blend of art and writing. Allow students' art to inform their written-language projects, and they will look forward to each new writing assignment.

Using the art they create, students begin writing from a high-interest starting point with concrete visual details—and their ideas flow onto the page. Sometimes they simply write what they see. They also may tell their story, poem, memoir, news account, or "how-to" piece with less difficulty and with much more enjoyment. The art students create helps give their writing a personal voice and lets them feel their writing is important and purposeful.

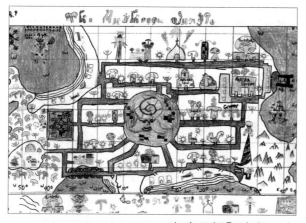

by Angelo P., sixth grade

How to Use This Book

Awesome Art Projects That Spark Super Writing is organized according to traditional forms of writing: narrative, expository, persuasive, and descriptive. For each activity, there is one page of teaching material and one reproducible student activity page. In the teaching material, you'll find additional form-specific points to review with students, and on pages 8 and 9, you'll find tips to share with students for successfully approaching each form of writing. The teaching pages also indicate whether the project is best suited for individual or group work.

In addition to the form-specific points, the teaching pages include a list of skills students will practice during the project, step-by-step directions, and student art and writing samples. Some activities offer an "extra dimension," or opportunities to take the learning a bit deeper. When these activities suggest using a Web site, please note that at the time this book went to press, the Web site addresses were correct. It's always important to preview each site to make sure the site is still active and that material is suitable for the developmental level of your students.

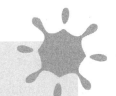

What the Research Shows

Over the years, research has supported using the arts to strengthen Language Arts and student learning.

✦ Gardner (1983) noted that students' learning styles may be far ranging and feature various strengths. He included spatial intelligence and an arts orientation as an important learning style for some students.

✦ Cortines (1999) suggested that arts projects build the types of thinking skills that leading corporations will need from their workers in the twenty-first century.

✦ Marzano et al. (2001) indicated that metaphors and analogies are among the best practices that can positively boost student achievement by as much as 45 percent. Clearly, student art—which in itself can be a metaphor—may well play an important role in building achievement.

✦ Barton et al. (2007) identified the arts as a way to nurture and enhance abstract thought within a literacy curriculum, so necessary for complex thinking and problem solving.

Awesome Art Projects That Spark Super Writing stems from these concepts.

Each student page comes with step-by-step directions, a project checklist, and cross-curricular ways to extend learning. Prior to each project, be sure to review the list of materials on the student page and gather enough supplies to meet the needs of your class. In a few cases, students must provide some of the materials.

by Joseph R., eighth grade

Where relevant, there are suggested word counts to help students write an appropriate amount. Please feel free to adapt these to suit the needs of your class. You may want to encourage students to present their writing double-spaced; typed, if possible.

Remind students to refer to the project checklists. These will offer quick reminders and guidance concerning each project to help students turn in their best work. These checklists include points related to the writing form and to specific elements of the project. They also include a target word count. Please feel free to amend these as necessary.

Most of these art-and-writing assignments work well as one-week projects, requiring approximately 45–50 minutes per day. For example, on the first day or two, students concentrate on the art. Days three and four are dedicated to the assignment's writing portion. Typically, the assignments are due at the end of the fifth working day, which gives students time for any last-minute art changes or editing. If students need more time, consider extending the due date. Some students will appreciate having the weekend to finish their work.

by Christopher B., sixth grade

If possible, try to build in time for students to share. Students are typically proud to share their work. If class time is at a premium, use your classroom selection process to allow five students or student-groups to share their projects. Give up to five minutes each.

If space is available, consider displaying students' art and writing in the classroom or school hallway. Exhibiting artistic and written works in school can boost students' reading enjoyment and visual literacy.

Teaching Tips

Introduce each assignment with art—You may find it helpful to introduce each assignment by showing famous artwork or any samples that you or students have already created that relate to the lesson's concept. For example, it is easy to find images of labyrinths and mazes online or in books and magazines to open the Great Labyrinth lesson (pages 10–11). These pictures, along with students' subsequent research, may help fire up their imaginations and become a bridge from the lesson concept to their own artistic creations.

Model writing by sharing your thoughts—Typically, students understand better when they see a teacher sharing ideas and showing how an assignment is to be done. When it comes to writing a persuasive argument, try sharing your thought process as you write from a student perspective. Think aloud: "I'd like to convince my teacher to let me change seats. So, I need to tell her why that's a good thing. If she says no, then I need to have a counterargument. Here's how I'll begin my writing: *Ms. Brown, if you allow me to change seats, I'll be more productive in class. I'll have fewer distractions around me. Since I work well with Veronica, if I sit near her, we'll be able to pair up for projects.*"

Refocus when necessary—During class time, students will create artwork first and then write. Whether students work independently or in groups, they are bound to become distracted from time to time and lose focus. That's why it may be helpful to say something like the following: "OK, let's restart, rethink, refocus, and review." Be sure to encourage students not to give up: "Let's do our best work for five more minutes. Then, we'll take a break, and you may share your work with a classmate."

Sandwich challenges between compliments—As you review student works in progress, you may choose to praise, challenge, and then praise again: "That's super line quality, Gabriel. Try adding more color here. Your composition is balanced and pleasing." Or, "I like your strong introduction. Please review spelling and use of commas. You've added lots of humor here, Lucille." While this is sometimes difficult to do on the fly, using a "sandwich" approach provides an opportunity to be specific and to guide students toward improving their art and writing.

Try an individual or small-group wrap-up—Once an assignment is complete and graded, students will benefit from a mini-conference with you. Showing a grading rubric, sharing a favorite part of the writing, suggesting future improvements, and asking thoughtful questions of students make for an effective and personal ending to the lesson.

Writing Form Tips

Narrative—Craft a coherent story

A coherent story means that the action holds together and makes sense for the reader. To craft a coherent story, students should make certain they

- ✦ Show the reader what a character is doing and thinking.
- ✦ Keep the plot simple and uncomplicated, with only two or three major story events.
- ✦ Use verbs in the proper tense:
  - Stories that are happening now use present-tense verbs.
  - Use past-tense verbs for action that happened in the past.
  - Add future-tense verbs for action that will occur.
- ✦ Vary the beginnings of sentences.
- ✦ Use transitional words or phrases to signal new action or events.

Expository—Develop and support a main idea

Expository writing deals with facts or research. Students should begin their exposition with a topic sentence that tells the reader an interesting fact about the main idea. This is then followed by three sentences that give more details about the main idea. For example, in writing about the American Dream, one student might cite a recent school survey and state that many Americans, especially students at the school, predict future personal success and happiness. The student could support that idea with three sentences that offer more details. For example:

Students at our school believe they will succeed in the future because they are studying now to become a success. Some students say they will pursue such fields as law, entertainment, the arts, writing, science, and sports. These students also predict that future success in these fields will make them truly happy.

In expository writing, students should also

- ✦ Present their writing using a clear structure, such as sequential, compare and contrast, or cause and effect.
- ✦ Summarize, paraphrase, and use direct quotes.
- ✦ Cite sources properly.

Persuasive—Build a persuasive argument

Persuasive writing can be advertising, an editorial, a political speech, or even a discussion in which one wants to have his or her own way. Suppose a student wants an increase in his or her weekly allowance. Explain that parents or guardians may not be willing to grant the raise unless the student can explain why she needs it and what she will do to earn it, such as cleaning around the house or turning in homework on time. Students can build an argument in writing by predicting what the reader may object to—and then offering ideas to convince the reader (parent) to agree with the writer (student). Offer these suggestions:

✦ If the reader may object to an idea, add another reason why the suggestion is a good one.

✦ If available, statistics are an effective way to back up an argument: For example, "Surveys suggest that students who earn their allowance actually perform better in school." Remind students to cite their source.

✦ In a conclusion, recap briefly all the reasons that advance the point of view.

Descriptive—Create description using precise words

Descriptive writing shows the reader a particular place, person, or activity. Sometimes descriptive writing also expresses what a character is feeling. Encourage students to experiment with the shades of meaning of the words they choose.

✦ Students should use powerful verbs and precise adjectives to make reading descriptive writing fun. For example, it's not just "orange juice," it's "fresh orange juice." *Fresh* and *orange* are adjectives that describe the noun *juice*. To make the writing even more precise— it's "cold, fresh-squeezed orange juice in a frosty glass." This describes precisely what a writer wants the reader to see! Likewise, one could say, "She drank the orange juice." But it may be more interesting for the reader to see the action precisely: "Sage grabbed the frosty glass and guzzled the fresh-squeezed orange juice in three seconds flat!"

✦ Students can use a thesaurus or an online dictionary, such as www.dictionary.com, to gather precise and descriptive words for their writing. Suggest that they keep a list of these words handy and refer to it when they have a writing assignment.

✦ Students should tap into the five senses when they are writing a descriptive piece.

Great Labyrinth

Students begin this project by researching what a labyrinth is. A labyrinth can be used for an enjoyable walk or a meditative stroll. Often, the seeker enters the labyrinth with a problem and hopes to find a solution upon reaching its center.

Objectives

- Write a narrative account.
- Identify steps to present an idea and solve a problem.
- Edit for style and consistency.

Directions

1. Photocopy student directions and gather needed materials (see page 11).

2. Distribute directions and materials to students. Go over project expectations and remind students that the art they create will act as a prompt for a narrative writing piece that is an example of a fairy tale.

3. Review the fairy tale genre. A fairy tale, such as *Cinderella*, is often a brief and simple story that involves magical characters or events.

4. Describe the purpose and structure of a labyrinth.

   - If time is tight and students have few research resources at hand, develop a few PowerPoint slides that show examples of mazes or labyrinths.

   - As necessary, provide students with a photocopy of a simple maze and allow them to trace their way to the center.

5. Have students draw their own maze or labyrinth. Allow students to draw by hand or on a computer.

6. When it's time for students to write their fairy tale, remind them that the labyrinth should be an important part of the story.

7. Before students share their stories and art with the class, hold an editing workshop. Allow classroom partners to help the writer edit the story for style and consistency.

8. Finally, students present their labyrinth artwork and accompanying short story.

Extra Dimension: Invite students to make a 3-D model of their labyrinth or maze and include a how-to explanation of its creation. Encourage students to photograph the planning and building processes.

In a faraway land there lived a fair maiden named Elizabeth. Elizabeth was a well-behaved, good looking, smart, and thoughtful young girl about the age of 14. She was known as "the puzzle girl" because she was so smart she could figure out puzzles, mazes, and riddles very quickly, and everyone knew that. Life was as good as it gets for Elizabeth—so it seemed.

Excerpt from "The Puzzle Girl"
by Rachael H., eighth grade

Great Labyrinth

Directions

1. By hand or on a computer, draw your own labyrinth, or maze.

2. Reflect on the artwork you have created. Think about the purpose of the labyrinth.

3. Write a short narrative story that is up to 250 words. The labyrinth should be an important part of the story. Use the fairy tale genre and tell your story simply and clearly.

4. Trade papers with a partner to edit the story for style and consistency.

5. Be prepared to show your artwork and read your story in class.

Materials

- construction paper
- pencils, pens, or markers
- ruler

Choose one of the following ways to extend your learning:

Young Historian—Create a photo essay with captions that provides a history of the labyrinth. What is the history of a labyrinth or maze that may exist in your town?

Young Playwright—Does your story lend itself to drama? Revise the story, add dialogue, and present your work as a labyrinth play.

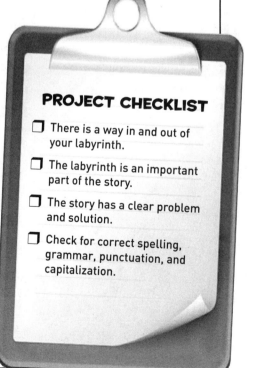

PROJECT CHECKLIST

☐ There is a way in and out of your labyrinth.

☐ The labyrinth is an important part of the story.

☐ The story has a clear problem and solution.

☐ Check for correct spelling, grammar, punctuation, and capitalization.

Found-Art Superhero

Students search their school, home, and neighborhood for interesting junk to use in found-object artwork. Next, they write an accompanying superhero story that features the objects they find.

Directions

1. Photocopy student directions and gather all materials, except the found-art objects (see page 13).

2. Distribute directions and materials to students. Go over project expectations. Be sure students understand that the art they create will act as a prompt for a narrative writing piece, involving a superhero.

3. Review the elements of narrative writing as necessary, such as using a variety of sentence structures. For example, students should vary the beginnings of their sentences. They should also use simple, compound, and complex sentences in their writing.

   • Typically, simple sentences are short: Garbage Guy saved the world with his "super junk."

   • Compound sentences are two simple sentences united with a conjunction and comma: Garbage Guy saved the world, and he used junk to do it.

   • Complex sentences use a dependent and an independent clause: Although the people were afraid, they had hope that Garbage Guy would save them.

4. Direct students to search their school, home, or neighborhood for interesting junk to bring in the following day. (Encourage them to search for up to 15–20 minutes and to wash the objects.)

5. Next, students create found-object artwork. (Give them one class period for this step.)

6. Then, invite students to write an accompanying superhero story that features their objects. The litter becomes an important element in the superhero story.

7. Invite students to share their art and writing with the class.

Objectives

• Craft a narrative by using found objects in creative ways.

• Sequence information to carry out a procedure.

• Use a variety of sentence structures.

Extra Dimension: Some students with access to a computer may wish to embed sound elements or effects into their story at appointed times. This enables the reader to hear sounds or music, adding an extra dimension to the superhero fun.

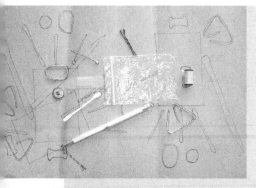

One day the Mouse Hero was running around the city to see if any animal was in trouble and in need of his help. Suddenly, he heard loud growls, followed by someone calling for help. So the Mouse Hero quickly went toward the sounds. When he got closer, he found a tall fence that he knew he could get over. He reached into his bag and pulled out a button and string. He tied the string around the button. He swung the string . . . and the button looped around one of the fence wires. The Mouse Hero then used the string to climb up the fence and down the other side. Then, he was back on his way to rescue whoever needed his help.

Excerpt from "The Mouse Hero" by Jessica M., eighth grade

Found-Art Superhero

Directions

1. Walk through your school or neighborhood (or search your home) to find ten discarded objects. Be sure to wash and dry them thoroughly.

2. Place the objects on a sheet of paper to form an interesting design or pattern. Use a pencil or marker to trace an outline of the objects.

3. Complete your artwork by gluing the found objects onto the construction paper.

4. Reflect on the artwork you have created. What does it say to you?

5. Next, write a short narrative story that is between 200 and 250 words. The story should focus on a superhero who uses these found objects to fight evil.

6. Give your story a beginning, middle, and end. (Consider making the story part of a series of stories involving your superhero.)

7. Trade papers with a partner to edit the story for style and consistency.

8. Be prepared to show your artwork and read your story in class.

Choose one of the following ways to extend your learning:

Young Mathematician—Which geometric shapes are present in the artwork? Calculate the angles.

Young Scientist—Take a survey of the types of litter and density of litter in a specific location. Analyze and report on your findings.

Materials

- 10 found-art objects (litter or refuse), washed
- construction paper
- tape, glue, or superglue
- pencils and colored markers

PROJECT CHECKLIST

- ☐ Superhero is original.
- ☐ Story includes references to the found objects.
- ☐ A problem is solved within the story.
- ☐ Story has a clear beginning, middle, and end.
- ☐ Check for correct spelling, grammar, punctuation, and capitalization.

Unique Universe

Students put a dark layer of black tempera paint over a multicolored crayon design. They scratch into the black with a stylus to create a line drawing, which reveals the many colors of the design underneath. This form becomes their universe in a night time sky and serves as the start of a story idea.

Objectives

- Invent a new universe to use as a story setting.
- Demonstrate proper tense usage.
- Write an introduction, body, and conclusion.

Directions

1. Photocopy student directions and gather needed materials (see page 15).

2. Distribute directions and materials to students. Go over project expectations and remind students that the art they create will act as a prompt for a narrative writing piece.

3. Review the elements of narrative writing as necessary, such as giving the story a clear beginning, middle, and end.

4. Have students draw a multicolored freeform design on construction paper using crayons. The crayons should cover all of the paper, and students should press hard to create full-intensity colors with crayons.

5. Once their paper is completely covered, direct students to use black tempera paint to cover over the first design.

6. Next, students should take a stylus, a pencil point, or a sharp object and draw into the black surface to create a universe of their choosing. A simple line drawing is effective and works well. The line drawing reveals many colors underneath the black.

   - For inspiration, you may also wish to share the "Constellations" series and other artwork by Joan Miró at www.artexpertswebsite.com/pages/artists/miro.php.

7. Finally, direct students to write a short story to accompany their artwork universe. Students can include themselves in their story or write about a fictional character.

by Rachael H., eighth grade

Adzuki was a lonely child. She rarely ever spoke, unless she needed something. People often mistook her for a ghost because of her moon-white skin and hair. But as quiet and as alone as she was, she had one thing that she was absolutely dazzled by. That dazzling thing was the stars.

Adzuki loved looking at the stars. She would stay up late (though she rarely ever slept anyway), pull out her children's telescope set, and watch the stars through her window. Through the thick palm trees outside growing from the island she watched them, each constellation that seemed to be passing her by.

"I must get closer to the stars," she said, clenching her fists and looking up. But first she had to learn *how* to get closer.

Excerpt from "The Stars" by Sydney P., eighth grade

Unique Universe

Directions

1. Draw a multicolored, freeform design on construction paper using crayons. The crayons should cover all of the paper. Be sure to press hard to create full-intensity colors with crayons.

2. Once the paper is completely covered, use black tempera paint to completely cover the first design.

3. Using a stylus or a pencil point, draw into the black surface to create a universe of your choosing. A simple line drawing is effective. It will reveal many colors underneath the black.

4. Write a short narrative story that is up to 250 words to accompany your artwork universe. Use the first-person "I" in your narrative if you wish.

5. Try to provide new information or a twist in plot during the middle of the story.

6. Trade papers with a partner to edit the story for style and consistency.

7. Be prepared to show your artwork and read your story in class.

Choose one of the following ways to extend your learning:

Young Scientist—Create a table that details similarities and differences between your imaginary universe and the Milky Way.

Young Actor or Actress—Act out a story that occurs in your imaginary universe. Write a brief analysis for your character.

Materials

- construction paper
- crayons
- black tempera paint
- stylus or sharp pencil point

PROJECT CHECKLIST

- ☐ Use the artwork as the setting for the narrative.
- ☐ The story has an interesting beginning.
- ☐ Provide interesting information or a plot twist, and end the story with an unexpected conclusion.
- ☐ Check for correct spelling, grammar, punctuation, and capitalization.

Our Town Gazette

Students invent a town and populate it with interesting characters. Then students create a newspaper for their imaginary town and publish the town's legends. The newspaper may also include headlines, art, captions, and a table of contents.

Objectives

- Write a legend containing conflict and resolution.
- Predict how the legend might be different if the group changed certain ideas.
- Respond to the fictional story by writing a short reflection essay.

Extra Dimension: Post the legend online at www.eastoftheweb.com or at another site that features student work.

Directions

1. Photocopy student directions and gather needed materials (see page 17).

2. Distribute directions and materials to students. Go over project expectations and remind students that the art they create will act as a prompt for a legend.

3. Review the elements of a legend as necessary. Legends explain how people or places began. While they may also be fairy tales or myths, legends tend to describe specific localities or individuals associated with a place. They may be viewed as a history that cannot be proved.

4. As a class, vote on a name for an imaginary town. Next, have students suggest up to 10 characters who live in the town. Divide the class into small groups. Each group will work with the same setting and characters.

5. Have student groups prepare a four-page tabloid that contains a legend of how the town began. They should include headlines, at least four stories, and draw pictures or enhance images found online. If available, encourage students to use computers and printers for a professional look.

6. Student may choose to reflect on the town and characters they created. What did they like best about the town? Which character was most popular and why?

7. Post the tabloids in the classroom. Have each group present its legend to the class.

Iceville tabloid
by Edith V.

the legend of iceville

Ice Ville all started when Mayor Jalac's great-great-great-great-great-great-great-great-grandfather discovered it. His name was Ice V. Ille and he was really the founder of the town. It has been said that he still haunts Ice Ville, but in a good way. As reporters Sam and Edith interviewed Mayor Jalac, he said that if he ever discovered a book with a legend of Ice Ville he would display it in his office—and that he was proud to be a mayor.

Excerpt from "The Legend of Ice Ville"
by Edith V., sixth grade

Our Town Gazette

Directions

1. Using the town name and list of characters the class selected as a group, prepare a four-page tabloid that contains a legend of how the town began.

2. Draw pictures or enhance images found online.

3. Write headlines and at least four stories. Each story should be between 50 and 150 words long.

4. Check for correct spelling, grammar, punctuation, and capitalization.

5. If available, use a computer and printer for a professional look. Then you can glue or tape the printed pages to newsprint or construction paper to create a larger tabloid.

6. Display your tabloid in the classroom and be prepared to present your legend to the class.

Materials

- newsprint or construction paper
- colored markers or crayons
- computer and printer access
- glue or tape

Choose one of the following ways to extend your learning:

Young Historian—Compare and contrast the legend about the founding of Rome with your own imaginary town legend.

Young Musician—Create a town anthem using percussive instruments.

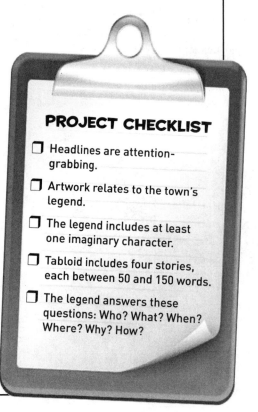

PROJECT CHECKLIST

☐ Headlines are attention-grabbing.

☐ Artwork relates to the town's legend.

☐ The legend includes at least one imaginary character.

☐ Tabloid includes four stories, each between 50 and 150 words.

☐ The legend answers these questions: Who? What? When? Where? Why? How?

Still-Life Spectacle

Students create a still life using watercolors from an inexpensive "dollar" store. Once complete, students write a dialogue that incorporates the still life in an interesting way. Students can add depth to their writing by giving their characters a dominant trait and attitude, including a physical description of the characters and setting.

Objectives

- Experiment with the qualities of watercolor.
- Use effective transition words.
- Write dialogue.

Extra Dimension: Encourage students to set up their own still life at home and photograph it under varied lighting conditions and locations. They should write a journal entry that explains how the photographs differ.

Directions

1. Photocopy student directions and gather needed materials (see page 19); 1–3 objects per student.

2. Show students a variety of still-life examples throughout art history. (Sister Wendy Beckett's art books are helpful here.)

3. If possible, allow students to search for still-life paintings online. Provide time for students to share their favorite still-life artworks with the class.

4. Distribute directions, watercolors, brushes, and paper. Invite students to practice with washes and brush techniques, such as drybrush. Show examples of washes, such as dark to light.

5. Go over project expectations. Remind students that the art they create will act as a prompt for a narrative writing piece that includes dialogue.

6. Review the elements of dialogue as necessary, particularly how to punctuate it correctly. Also, focus on how writers use transition words (now, then, next, for example, and so on) to keep a story flowing logically.

7. Ask students to choose 1–3 objects for the subject of their still-life watercolor. They may complete their watercolor at home (or in class, if time is available).

8. Have students write a narrative story that incorporates their watercolor.

The still life was almost finished, and the man had no idea what to do with all of the fruit that he had gathered. Meanwhile, the fruits themselves had no idea that they were on the man's mind.

"I don't care what you think; I'm the most tasty fruit in the world," said Banana, who was quite stuck up and arrogant.

"Whatever," replied Apple, who was a bit on the cocky side himself. "You know what they say: an apple a day keeps the doctor away."

"I'm the most juicy," said Orange, rather snobbishly.

"Will you all just shut up!" shouted a chorus of small voices coming from the sour Grapes.

Excerpt from "Fruit Pie" by Spencer B., eighth grade

Still-Life Spectacle

Directions

1. Select 1–3 objects for the subject of your still life.

2. Using watercolors and brushes, create a still-life painting. Think about your use of dark to light. Experiment with washes and brush techniques, such as drybrush.

3. When your watercolor is complete, write a creative story that is up to 500 words to accompany your artwork.

4. Include dialogue and transition words in your story.

5. Trade papers with a partner to edit the story for style and consistency.

6. Be prepared to show your artwork and read your story in class.

Choose one of the following ways to extend your learning:

Young Mathematician—View 12 still-life paintings and add up all the objects you see. What is the average number of objects per painting?

Young Athlete—Make an obstacle course using still-life objects. How fast can you run the course?

Materials

• construction paper
• watercolors and brushes
• 1–3 objects to form a still life

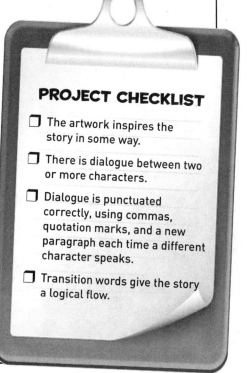

PROJECT CHECKLIST

☐ The artwork inspires the story in some way.

☐ There is dialogue between two or more characters.

☐ Dialogue is punctuated correctly, using commas, quotation marks, and a new paragraph each time a different character speaks.

☐ Transition words give the story a logical flow.

Torn-Paper Autobiography

Understanding the story of one's own life is an important part of adolescent identity and development. Students make a self-portrait from torn bits of colored paper and write their own life story.

Objectives

- Use a variety of sentence structures (simple, compound, complex) and types (declarative, interrogative, exclamatory, and imperative).

- Select effective formats for publication of the final product.

- Use available technology (laptop publishing, electronic dictionary, and printing).

Extra Dimension: To expand students' writing skills, have them interview someone in their family, such as a grandparent, and write a biography about that person.

Directions

1. Photocopy student directions and gather needed materials (see page 21).

2. Distribute directions and materials to students. Go over project expectations and remind students that the art they create will act as a prompt for an autobiography.

3. Show students some examples of torn-paper art, if possible, and review the elements of an autobiography as necessary, such as speaking candidly about oneself, mentioning important events that define one's life, and presenting ideas in a logical (often chronological) way.

4. Next, have students create their own self-portrait by gluing torn bits of construction paper onto one larger sheet of paper (on which they've already drawn their face, using a pen or pencil).

5. Then, students should write a five-paragraph autobiography. Remind students that they will share their autobiographies with the class so they should choose only those areas of their life they are comfortable revealing to others.

6. Encourage students to end with positive predictions for their future.

> When I look in the mirror, I see myself. I have long hair and glasses. I'm about 5' 3" tall, and I'm almost 12 years old. I like my sparkling brown eyes.
>
> Right now I am in Girl Scouts and it's so fun. We make crafts and play games. The other girls in the troop are so cool. They are fun and crazy in a good way (we all are). We go on trips like downtown to the Hyatt for the Christmas Light Parade.
>
> *Excerpt from "An Autobiography All About Me!"*
> *by Taylor O., sixth grade*

Torn-Paper Autobiography

Directions

1. To begin your self-portrait, choose construction paper colors for your face, eyes, hair, eyebrows, glasses, and other accessories.

2. Using a pen or pencil, draw your face on a sheet of construction paper. Next, tear the multicolored swatches into small bits.

3. Glue the paper bits over your pencil drawing to create a torn-paper portrait.

4. Write a five-paragraph factual account of your life that is up to 500 words to accompany your artwork. Be sure to share only those areas of your life that you are comfortable revealing to others.

5. Write about your important life experiences.

6. End with positive predictions for your own future.

7. Trade papers with a partner to edit for style and consistency.

8. Be prepared to show your artwork and read your autobiography in class.

Choose one of the following ways to extend your learning:

Young Librarian—Investigate autobiographies in your library. Choose two books, and compare and contrast them. Look for common and divergent themes.

Young Attorney—Read a biography about a famous lawyer. How did he/she advance, and which cases helped to make him/her famous?

Materials

- multicolored construction paper
- glue
- pencil or pen

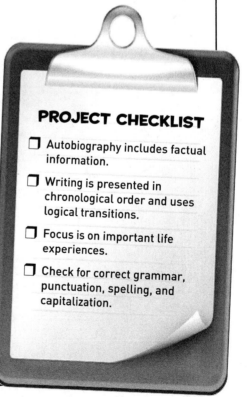

PROJECT CHECKLIST

☐ Autobiography includes factual information.

☐ Writing is presented in chronological order and uses logical transitions.

☐ Focus is on important life experiences.

☐ Check for correct grammar, punctuation, spelling, and capitalization.

Canned Art

Students decorate cans that will contain information on a historical figure they've studied and will write about.

Extra Dimension: Invite students to write a magazine feature article about the historical figure. Encourage them to use direct quotes of actual comments that person said.

Directions

1. Prior to the day you plan to do this project, ask students to bring in a washed soup can or a similar can from home.

2. Photocopy student directions and gather the rest of the needed materials (see page 23).

3. Distribute directions and materials to students. Go over project expectations and remind students that because the can they decorate will act as a container for important biographical information, decorations should relate to their subject.

4. Review the elements of a research project as necessary, such as using a variety of sources, sharing only the most important information, and putting that information into their own words. You may also want to go over the importance of citing sources and the proper way to cite various sources.

5. Invite students to choose a historical figure to study and begin to decorate the outside of their can with images related to the person.

6. Encourage students to add some 3-D objects and other items that represent the historical figure.

7. Direct students to write 20 questions and answers about the person on index cards. Depending on the size of the can, students may cut the cards in half so they fit inside the can easily. For example, if they are focusing on a world leader, suggest that students ask one important question about the leader's youth on one index card and one question about his or her time in power on another. Students should write the answers on the reverse side.

8. Using the information they've gathered on index cards, have students reflect on what they've learned and write a biographical essay on the historical figure, sharing the details about this person that interested them the most.

9. Once they have completed their essay, have students tie the cards together using colorful yarn, roll essay into a scroll, and tie it with a ribbon, placing both inside the can.

10. Students should include an image of the historical figure, if available, or draw one.

Titles given to Rosa Parks were "The Patron Saint," "The Spark That Lit the Fire," and "The Mother of the Movement."
Excerpt from "Ten Facts About Rosa Parks" by Sairis P., sixth grade

Canned Art

Directions

1. Choose a person from history you would like to study.

2. Decorate the outside of a can with images of your subject if available. Add some 3-D objects, if possible, and other words or items that represent your historical figure.

3. Print out or draw an image of your subject and attach it to a craft stick. Put the stick inside the can so the image can be seen.

4. On individual index cards, write 20 questions and answers about the person you are studying. Write the question one side and the answer to the question on the reverse side. Remember to cite your sources on each card.

5. Using the information you've gathered on the index cards, reflect on what you've learned. Write a biographical essay between 200 and 250 words on the historical figure, sharing the details that interested you.

6. When the essay is complete, roll it into a scroll, tie it with a ribbon, and add it to the can. Be sure to tie the cards together using colorful yarn, and drop them inside the can.

7. Be prepared to describe your canned art and read your essay in class.

Materials

- empty can, washed
- craft stick
- 20 3" x 5" index cards
- colorful yarn
- pictures
- glue
- ribbon
- colored markers

Choose one of the following ways to extend your learning:

Young Musician—Write a song about your historical figure and include facts from your index cards.

Young Historian—Pretend you are the historical figure that you researched. Share your life story through an autobiography or an oral presentation.

PROJECT CHECKLIST

☐ Images on can relate to historical figure and the picture of your subject is visible when it is inside the can.

☐ Each question is answered in a complete sentence.

☐ Each index card contains a citation.

☐ Check for correct spelling, grammar, punctuation, and capitalization.

I'm "Board"

Students study games and then design and create their own board game about some aspect of writing, such as grammar, punctuation, creating a story, poetry, and so forth.

Directions

1. Photocopy student directions (see page 25). For this project, students are responsible for gathering and bringing to school all needed materials.

2. Have students bring a board game to class. Students play the games in class during language arts. As they play, students make a list of the many elements such a game may contain, such as a board, playing pieces, cards, rules, money, and so on.

3. Distribute directions and go over project expectations. Remind students that the board game they create will convey information related to language arts—on a topic that you approve such as building complete sentences, identifying parts of speech, and so on.

4. Show students examples of game directions, if possible. Review the elements of "how-to" writing as necessary, such as explaining the steps involved in a process, activity, or game; making certain all the steps are described thoroughly; and writing simply and clearly for readers.

5. Direct students to name the game, and decide how to play and win.

6. Next, students create a colorful board, write the game rules, make playing pieces, and add whatever else is necessary to play the game successfully.

7. Then, have different student groups play the game and comment on it. (Students may need to make changes to their game, as recommended by the other student groups that played it.)

8. End the project with a final day of game-playing fun!

Objectives

- Work effectively in groups.
- Design a project with an objective and problem solving.
- Demonstrate English language conventions.

Extra Dimension: Encourage students to design a container to house their game.

Athena R., Omar R., and Angelo P., sixth grade, give their language arts game a try. Creating language arts board games helps students to recall what they have learned and strengthens their long-term memory.

I'm "Board"

Directions

1. Think of any board games you have played. Make a list of the many elements such a game may contain.

2. Using some or all of these elements, create a board game that focuses on a language arts topic.

3. Think of a name for your game.

4. Decide how to play and win it.

5. If your game includes questions, be sure there are both easy and difficult ones to answer.

6. Create a colorful board, make playing pieces, write the game rules, and make whatever else is necessary to play the game successfully.

7. Trade games with other students and play each other's games. Be prepared to discuss what you learned about the topic by playing the game.

Choose one of the following ways to extend your learning:

Young Poet—Help others learn about poetic terminology, poets, and the making of poems by creating a poetic board game.

Young Mathematician—Giving answers to math problems in addition, subtraction, multiplication, and division could be among the questions in a math-related game.

Materials

- colored posterboard (one per person or group)
- colored pencils and markers

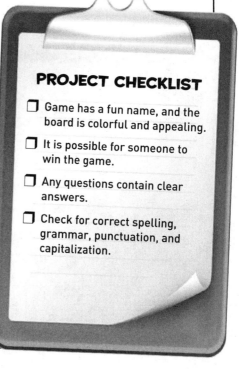

PROJECT CHECKLIST

☐ Game has a fun name, and the board is colorful and appealing.

☐ It is possible for someone to win the game.

☐ Any questions contain clear answers.

☐ Check for correct spelling, grammar, punctuation, and capitalization.

Artistic Anachronism

Students observe a portrait from a historical time period, draw it, and then add something contemporary to the portrait. This is a fun and colorful project for students, who will enjoy adding humor to their work.

Directions

1. Photocopy student directions and gather needed materials (see page 27).

2. Distribute directions and materials to students. Go over project expectations and let students know that they will illustrate a rendition of a classic painting. Remind them that the art they create will act as a prompt for an expository writing piece.

3. Review the elements of expository writing, such as note-taking of factual/ historical information, identifying important historical or biographical events, and revising the notes to avoid plagiarism.

4. Next, invite students to find a famous portrait in an art book or search for one online.

5. Have them do their best to draw the portrait and add color to it.

6. Before they are finished with the artwork, remind students to add something contemporary to the drawing, such as a candy bar, soda can, a computer, or other electronic device.

7. Finally, direct students to write a five-paragraph essay that relates in some way to the classic painting. For example, the essay could focus on the life and achievements of the painting's subject or the artist, or the importance of a historical period or place.

Objectives

- Develop an organized essay in five paragraphs.

- Research material and paraphrase information.

- Investigate how art reflects different cultures, times, and places.

Extra Dimension: Compare and contrast a historical period with modern times.

In 1534, Sir Thomas More was sent to the Tower after continually refusing to support the king. The next year was his last. On July 1, in the year 1535, Sir Thomas More was convicted of treason. On July 6, he was beheaded on Tower Hill. Because of his bravery and martyrdom, he was canonized by Pope Pius XI in May of 1935. Saint Thomas More is an excellent example of standing up to people for what you believe in and making the right choice when there are moral decisions to make.

Excerpt from "Sir Thomas More" by Emily A., seventh grade

Artistic Anachronism

Directions

1. Find a famous portrait in an art book or search for one online. Notice how the portrait reflects the era it comes from.

2. Do your best to draw the portrait and add color to it if necessary.

3. Before you are finished with the artwork, remember to add something contemporary to the drawing, such as a candy bar, soda can, a computer, or other electronic device.

4. Use at least two sources to research and take notes about a historical person, period, or place that relates to the artwork.

5. Using your notes, write a five-paragraph essay that is about 250 words. Be sure to include an introduction, three factual paragraphs for the body of the essay, and a one-paragraph conclusion. The contemporary element should be part of the essay.

6. Trade papers with a partner to edit the essay for style and consistency.

7. Be prepared to show your artwork and read your essay in class.

Choose one of the following ways to extend your learning:

Young Historian—Among the famous women and men you have studied, how many of them have online portraits that you can study? What do portraits tell you about these people that facts do not?

Young Mathematician—How many different geometric shapes can you find within a portrait? Highlight or outline them.

Materials

- construction paper
- crayons and markers

PROJECT CHECKLIST

❏ Historical portrait includes a modern accessory.

❏ Five-paragraph essay includes an introduction, three paragraphs of factual information, and a conclusion.

❏ Essay cites your sources.

❏ Check for correct spelling, grammar, punctuation, and capitalization.

Frog Focus

Students love to draw animals, especially colorful frogs! Once their artwork is complete, have students write an expository piece that involves the frogs they drew, and that contains one or more nonfiction text features.

Directions

1. Photocopy student directions and gather needed materials (see page 29).

2. Distribute directions and materials to students. Go over project expectations and let students know that the art they create will act as a prompt for an expository writing piece that includes factual information about frogs.

3. Review the elements of expository writing, including text features such as sidebars, headings, captions, graphs, and maps.

4. Next, have students investigate frogs online and read picture books about them. Check out books from your school or local library, as necessary.

5. Then, students draw, color, and label at least two of their favorite frogs.

6. Students incorporate their drawings into a mini-report. Each student should write a sidebar of "Fascinating Facts About Frogs." Encourage students to incorporate other nonfiction text features. Remind them to cite the sources they used to write their reports.

Objectives

- Compose expository writing that supports a topic with evidence.

- Establish personal style and voice.

- Cite the source of direct quotations and summarized information.

Extra Dimension: Invite students to transform their artwork into a color-by-numbers image so anyone can re-create the frogs they chose.

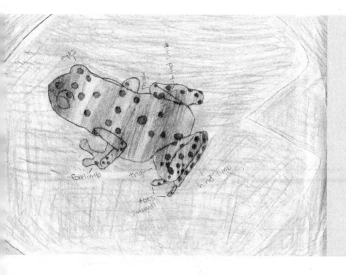

♦ Frogs prefer to live in moist areas. They live in ponds, creeks, and trees.

♦ Frogs don't drink water. They absorb it through their skin.

♦ There are more than 4,000 species of frogs in the world.

♦ Only nine species of frogs are poisonous.

Excerpt from "Fascinating Facts About Frogs," by Tara M., seventh grade

Frog Focus

Directions

1. Investigate frogs online and read picture books about them. Check out books from your school or local library, if needed.

2. Next, draw, color, and label at least two of your favorite frogs.

3. Write a mini-report about these frogs. Be sure to include a sidebar of "Fascinating Facts About Frogs."

4. Use other nonfiction text features in your writing, such as headings or bold text for unfamiliar vocabulary.

5. Remember to cite the sources you used to write your report.

6. Trade papers with a partner to edit the report for style and consistency.

7. Be prepared to show your artwork and read parts of your report in class.

Materials

- construction paper
- markers and crayons

Choose one of the following ways to extend your learning:

Young Writer—Create your own picture book about one frog's life.

Young Reader—Which stories about frogs do you like best and why? Keep your comments in a book review journal, online file, or blog.

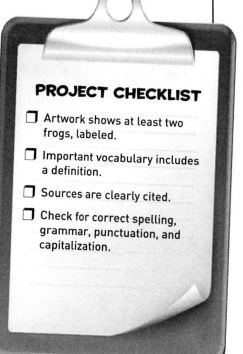

PROJECT CHECKLIST

☐ Artwork shows at least two frogs, labeled.

☐ Important vocabulary includes a definition.

☐ Sources are clearly cited.

☐ Check for correct spelling, grammar, punctuation, and capitalization.

Brilliant Biography

Students research the life of an important historical figure and make a colorful mini-poster of ten facts they found noteworthy. This is a simple classroom exercise that enhances student ability to paraphrase both major and minor details and list them in chronological order.

Objectives

- Compare and contrast information from various sources.
- Demonstrate responsibility to work for the common good of society.
- List social-justice themes present in the lives of notable leaders in a variety of disciplines.

Directions

1. Photocopy student directions and gather needed materials (see page 31).

2. Distribute directions and materials to students. Go over project expectations and let students know that the art they create will serve as a prompt for an expository writing piece that includes factual information about an important historical figure.

3. Review the elements of expository writing, such as the different text structures authors may use to present information. Point out that for this project students will use sequence—a text structure that will help them place key information in chronological order.

4. Have students choose an important figure from history, literature, science, or mathematics.

5. Next, direct students to research biographical data about the person, keeping notes on important information.

6. Then, students choose at least ten facts that they believe are the most important. They should paraphrase the information and list the facts in chronological order.

7. Finally, students incorporate the facts in a neat and colorful manner in a poster.

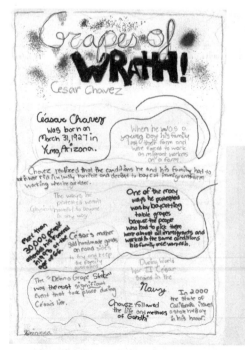

♦ One of the many ways he protested was by boycotting table grapes because the people who had to pick them were almost all immigrants and worked in the same ridiculously horrible conditions his family once worked in.

♦ The ways he protested weren't (physically) harmful to anyone in any way. Chavez followed the life and methods of Gandhi.

Excerpt from "Grapes of Wrath: Cesar Chavez"
by Brianna O., seventh grade

Brilliant Biography

Directions

1. Choose an important figure from history, literature, science, or mathematics.

2. Next, research biographical data about the person, taking precise notes on important information. (Be sure to keep track of your sources and include citations.)

3. Then, choose at least ten facts that you believe are the most important.

4. Paraphrase the information. Write a total of about 250 words.

5. Place the facts in chronological order.

6. Add the facts to a poster in a neat and colorful manner.

7. Trade posters with a partner to edit the essay for style and consistency.

8. Be prepared to show your artwork and share important facts in class.

Materials

- construction paper
- colored pencils and markers

Choose one of the following ways to extend your learning:

Young Historian—Create a real-life "wax museum" of leading figures in the arts or sciences. Dress as one of these leaders and be prepared to discuss his or her achievements.

Young Biographer—Prepare a PowerPoint biographical presentation about a leader in the arts or sciences.

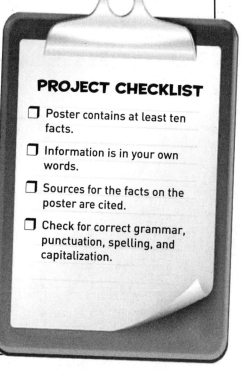

PROJECT CHECKLIST

- ☐ Poster contains at least ten facts.
- ☐ Information is in your own words.
- ☐ Sources for the facts on the poster are cited.
- ☐ Check for correct grammar, punctuation, spelling, and capitalization.

Research Paper

While a research paper can appear daunting at first, some students will appreciate beginning the process by using their imagination to draw a whimsical and interesting cover about their chosen topic. The creative cover of their research paper may help keep them inspired during the subsequent research and writing.

Objectives

- Develop a thesis statement or major question to be answered in the paper.
- Organize subject matter in a logical fashion.
- Cite sources within a bibliography.

Extra Dimension: Encourage students to create a speech based on their research and give a five-minute presentation. The speech could also explain the steps taken to research and write the paper, and students might also show the class their report cover and bibliography.

Directions

1. Photocopy student directions and gather needed materials (see page 33).

2. Distribute directions and materials to students. Go over project expectations and let students know that they will illustrate a cover for their research paper. Remind them that the art they create will serve as inspiration as they research their topic.

3. Review the elements of expository writing, such as how to organize the subject matter. Point out that there are a variety of ways to structure their presentation, depending on the topic. They may want to use chronological order, or focus on comparing and contrasting key information.

4. Next, students should choose a topic to research and develop a thesis statement. For example, a student who wishes to write about poet Robert Frost may investigate the role of nature as a metaphor for human feelings and emotions within Frost's poems.

5. Invite students to create a visually pleasing report cover that centers on their imaginative impressions about the subject.

6. Have them find three or four Web sites, books, or other resources for research on the topic.

7. Students will use index cards to note important research findings, then write a one- to five-page paper on the subject, including a bibliography that cites research sources. (Suggested minimum word count by grade: fourth, 200; fifth, 400; sixth, 600; seventh, 800; eighth, 1,000.)

by Melanie V., seventh grade

Emily has done a good job of explaining her messages through the feeling words in her poems and stories. Her writings can move you from head to toe; they can bring you to tears and make your heart pound with the touching phrases.

Excerpt from "Who Is Emily Bronte?"
by Marylou R., eighth grade

Research Paper

1. Choose a topic that interests you most. Consider writing about your favorite author, subject in school, or hobby.

2. Use your imagination to visualize your topic as a report cover. Show action on the cover if you can.

3. Create a thesis statement or attempt to answer an important question about your topic.

4. Use a computer to search at least three resources that may answer your question or relate to your thesis statement.

5. Take notes about the most interesting information you find. Record these facts and ideas on note cards.

6. Organize the note cards so that the order of the information will make sense to the reader. Then begin to write a paper in an organized way. Write clearly so the reader can understand what your research means. Be certain to answer the major question you researched.

7. Include a bibliography that lists the Web sites and other research sources you used. This goes at the end of your paper.

Materials

- paper
- crayons and markers
- note cards

Choose one of the following ways to extend your learning:

Young Librarian—Did you find a book, magazine, or DVD about your topic that isn't in your local library? If so, mention it to your librarian and suggest the library acquire it.

Young Researcher—List all the books, Web sites, magazine articles, and blogs that relate to your research paper topic. How many sources did you find?

PROJECT CHECKLIST

- ☐ Report cover art relates to your topic.
- ☐ Paper has a thesis statement or major question to answer.
- ☐ Information comes from at least three resources, cited correctly.
- ☐ Check for correct spelling, grammar, punctuation, and capitalization.

Shakespeare at the Movies

Students create a movie poster for one of Shakespeare's plays. The artwork serves as the report cover for a five-page paper in which students use persuasive writing skills to suggest that the play still speaks to contemporary readers and audiences.

Objectives

- Interpret and analyze text.

- Compare/contrast a text with contemporary events or societal values.

- Persuade readers that the age-old themes of a Shakespeare play, such as power, greed, deception, and guilt, are relevant in today's world.

Extra Dimension: Design a postcard or e-card that contains the report cover on one side and on the reverse a three-paragraph explanation (about 150 words) of what the cover means.

Directions

1. Photocopy student directions and gather needed materials (see page 35).

2. To help take some of the mystery out of a Shakespeare play you are studying (such as *Macbeth*, *Romeo and Juliet*, or *The Taming of the Shrew*), find some movie clips of the play online and share them with students. Ask students to comment on what they notice about the sets, costumes, and so on.

3. Next, distribute directions and materials to students. Go over project expectations and remind students that the art they create will act as a prompt for a persuasive writing piece.

4. Review the elements of persuasive writing as necessary, such as outlining and defending an argument, and including a counterargument.

5. Invite students to consider the major themes in the Shakespearean play they are reading, and draw a movie poster that would help someone who is not familiar with the play understand what it is all about.

6. Encourage students to use symbols to highlight the themes, or draw characters and props that are important to the play.

7. Students should then write a one- to five-page persuasive paper (see suggested minimum word count on page 32) arguing that the play overall relates to society today, highlighting relevant key themes and character motivations. You may want students to focus on one scene. In this case, students should write about 200 words.

This scene is about unchecked ambitions and the troubles one will go through to achieve dreams and ambitions. Macbeth, who killed people to get what he and his wife wanted, suddenly felt guilty and needed guidance and answers to eat back at his guilt. It is almost as if Macbeth is trying to believe something so hard that he is manipulating himself into believing what he wants to believe.

In this play Shakespeare put regret and reflection into Macbeth's character. It contains thoughts and emotions that can be compared to those of today's people.

Excerpt from an analysis of Macbeth, Act 2, Scene 2,
by Mady S., eighth grade

Shakespeare at the Movies

Directions

1. After reading one of Shakespeare's plays, consider its major themes.

2. Create a report cover in the style of a movie poster.

3. Try to use symbols to highlight the themes, or draw characters and props that are important to the play. The image should help someone who is not familiar with the play understand what it is all about.

4. Write a persuasive paper that shows the significance of the play for today's society. Be sure to address relevant key themes and character motivations, and defend your argument.

5. Review and edit the paper with a peer.

Materials

- construction paper
- markers and crayons

Choose one of the following ways to extend your learning:

Young Librarian—How many books by or about Shakespeare are in your school or local library? Choose ten that interest you and categorize them by topic or genre.

Young Movie Critic—How does the book or play differ from the film version of the same story? Keep a notebook of differences you see.

Young Actor or Actress—Memorize a soliloquy from the play you studied and present it to the class. Be ready to explain what it all means.

PROJECT CHECKLIST

- ❏ Paper highlights at least one universal theme.
- ❏ Writing includes an analysis of theme, characters, and motivations.
- ❏ Report cover looks like a movie poster.
- ❏ Examples from the text support your argument.
- ❏ Check for correct spelling, grammar, punctuation, and capitalization.

Positive-Negative Design

In this project, students express both the negative and positive aspects of space in their designs. Their artwork becomes a metaphor for the negative and positive story they tell. In their writing, students may focus on negative events. However, you should encourage them to end their stories in a positive manner, one that stresses peace and hope.

Objectives

- Write a powerful, organized persuasive story with a point of view.

- Explore two sides of an issue.

- Determine whether plot events are positive or negative.

Directions

1. Photocopy student directions and gather needed materials (see page 37).

2. Distribute directions and materials to students. Go over project expectations and remind students that the art they create will act as a prompt for a persuasive writing piece.

3. Review the elements of persuasive writing as necessary, such as taking a stand on an issue and being able to explain why.

4. Next, show students examples of positive and negative space in artwork. Positive space is a person or object that takes up space in the art. Negative space, for example, is an "empty" background. Use a search engine to find positive-negative designs or see www.carolynrobertsart.com/posneg.html for a lesson on creating these designs.

5. Direct students to create their own positive-negative designs using construction paper, colored pencils, and markers.

6. Give students time to reflect on their art. Ask them to prepare a list of ideas, images, and events they see in the artwork they drew.

7. Using the artwork and the list, have students write a persuasive story that contains both positive and negative occurrences. If possible, students should end the story on a positive note, recalling the saying, "Every cloud has a silver lining."

There were thousands of stars. Not dim or ones that you could barely see, but ones you could see from thousands of miles away. This was the kind of place I wish I could live forever. I must have fallen asleep because I woke up in my bed. I looked around waiting to go back to that dream world, but I didn't. I realized I had gotten a chance to be at a place where the stars were the most beautiful.

Excerpt from "Where the Stars Are the Most Beautiful"
by Katy W., eighth grade

Positive-Negative Design

Directions

1. Create a positive-negative design using construction paper, colored pencils, crayons, or markers.

2. Take some time to reflect on your art. Next, prepare a list of ideas, images, and events you see in your artwork.

3. Try to focus on a simple image to symbolize a viewpoint on a topic you think is worth taking a stand on.

4. Using the artwork and the list, write a short story up to 250 words that contains both positive and negative occurrences. In your story, try to persuade the reader to support your viewpoint.

5. If possible, end the story on a positive note. Think about the saying "Every cloud has a silver lining." Explain how this is true in your story.

6. Trade papers with a partner to edit the story for style and consistency.

7. Be prepared to show your artwork and read your story in class.

Choose one of the following ways to extend your learning:

Young Historian—Think of an event in world history that can be seen as positive. Can the same event be seen as negative? Why or why not?

Young Linguist—Devise a list of synonyms and antonyms to describe what you created within your positive and negative artwork.

Materials

- construction paper
- crayons, markers, or colored pencils

PROJECT CHECKLIST

- ☐ Artwork includes both positive and negative space.
- ☐ Viewpoint is clearly stated.
- ☐ Story shows why the viewpoint merits support.
- ☐ Check for correct spelling, grammar, punctuation, and capitalization.

Awesome Art Projects That Spark Super Writing • Copyright © 2011 by Jan Wiezorek, Scholastic Teaching Resources

Teen Catalog

Students create a four-page catalog with an attractive cover, multiple images, product descriptions, and an order form. Their catalogs should advertise products that interest teens, such as movies, video games, new technology, fashion, and more. This project involves students in both nonfiction and persuasive writing and challenges them to rewrite the material they research online.

Objectives

- Write text and select graphic materials to present information.

- Accommodate the characteristics of your audience as you persuade them.

- Use text and art effectively for a specific purpose.

Directions

1. Photocopy student directions and gather needed materials (see page 39). Decide whether students will create their catalogs on a computer or by hand.

2. Distribute directions and materials to students. Go over project expectations and remind students that the purpose of the catalog they create is to persuade their market—teens—to buy the products inside.

3. Next, show students examples of various catalogs. Be sure to show examples of an order form. Discuss the similarities. Ask them to describe what makes them want to buy a product.

4. Then, have students choose one theme or topic for their teen catalog and begin to research available products.

5. Direct them to design a cover (for page 1), select images or draw illustrations of products, and write persuasive paragraphs about the products (for pages 2 and 3).

6. Remind them to create an order form to place on page 4.

7. Finally, have students publish their catalogs. If possible, allow time for other students to "shop" from their classmates' catalogs.

*by Fredrick B.,
sixth grade*

♦ Stretchy belts like these are good for dresses that are floppy and long, giving them more style.

♦ This shirt has spunk and style! It is perfect for a day out at the beach, especially if you're on a boat.

*Excerpts from the "Girl Weekly" clothing catalog
by Jennifer O. and Helen D., seventh grade*

Teen Catalog

Directions

1. Choose one theme or topic for your teen catalog. Begin to research available products.

2. Think about what you might want to include in your catalog. Imagine what your catalog will look like. How will it get people's attention?

3. Next, design a cover (page 1), select images or draw illustrations of products.

4. Write persuasive paragraphs about the products (for pages 2 and 3).

5. Remember to create an order form to place on page 4.

6. Finally, publish your catalog. What products do fellow students seem to be most interested in buying?

Materials

- assorted markers, crayons, and colored pencils
- construction paper

Choose one of the following ways to extend your learning:

Young Nutritionist—Make a catalog of healthful snacks, such as fruits and vegetables, and find ways, using persuasive writing, to make them more appealing than junk food.

Young Marketer—Using either a product from your catalog or a new item, write and design an advertising brochure to entice students to buy your product.

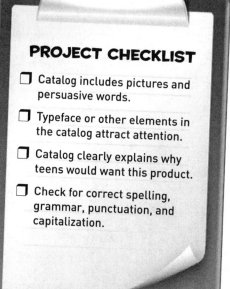

PROJECT CHECKLIST

- ☐ Catalog includes pictures and persuasive words.
- ☐ Typeface or other elements in the catalog attract attention.
- ☐ Catalog clearly explains why teens would want this product.
- ☐ Check for correct spelling, grammar, punctuation, and capitalization.

Commercial Storyboard

Students think of a product and create a commercial storyboard that includes camera angles, art, and written descriptions of the scenes.

Directions

1. Photocopy student directions and gather needed materials (see page 41).

2. Distribute directions and materials to students. Go over project expectations and remind students that the purpose of the commercial they plan is to persuade their market—preteens—to want to buy the products they see.

3. Next, review storyboards with students. Explain that they are used to help people visualize how a product advertisement will appear—before it is actually produced. It can include both images and words.

   • Study cinematic terms at www.filmsite.org/filmterms1.html.

   • View classic television commercials at www.archive.org/details/ClassicT1948.

4. Once they understand the concept, have students think of a product that preteens might want to buy.

5. Then, students should devise a storyboard to advertise the product. Remind them to include visuals and words in the storyboard.

Objectives

• Use new vocabulary.

• Select an effective format for publication of the final product.

• Write creatively for a specified purpose and audience.

Extra Dimension: Use a digital movie camera to record and then play the commercial for the class.

"High Angle"

This is a high angle of two friends who were ready for a party. One of the girls wanted to use CoCofume, so she asked her friend.

In this commercial storyboard for "CoCofume," Gendell F., seventh grade, describes a scene shot from a high angle. The frame shows two friends who are ready for a party. One of the girls wants to use CoCofume, so she asks to borrow her friend's bottle.

Commercial Storyboard

Directions

1. Think of a product that preteens might want to buy.

2. Devise a storyboard to advertise the product. Remember to include camera angles and any narration or dialogue for your commercial in the storyboard.

3. Pair up with another student and look at each other's storyboards. Describe all the ways the commercial is designed to persuade viewers to buy the product.

4. Be prepared to show your storyboard in class and explain how your advertisement will persuade preteens to buy the product.

Choose one of the following ways to extend your learning:

Young Linguist—How could students learn new vocabulary words by watching your commercial?

Young Inventor—Is your product a new invention? How does it work and who would benefit from it?

Materials

- paper
- pencils, colored markers, and crayons

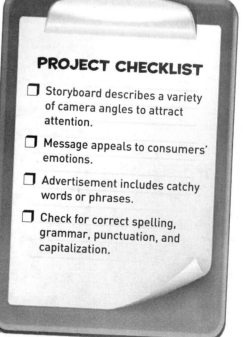

PROJECT CHECKLIST

☐ Storyboard describes a variety of camera angles to attract attention.

☐ Message appeals to consumers' emotions.

☐ Advertisement includes catchy words or phrases.

☐ Check for correct spelling, grammar, punctuation, and capitalization.

Earth Day, Hurrah!

Students celebrate Earth Day by creating posters with slogans and researching facts about saving our planet. Then, on Earth Day, they can march around the school and make passersby aware of the importance of working for a cleaner world. They can also take sidewalk chalk and write planet-saving facts for others to read.

Objectives

- Interrelate material from language arts, science, math, and reading.
- Write headlines and sentences to call attention to important concepts.
- Use physical activity to help make learning memorable.

Extra Dimension: Ask a speaker from a neighborhood action group to discuss ways in which students can participate in recycling and in making lifestyle changes for a better environment.

Directions

1. Photocopy student directions and gather needed materials (see page 43).

2. Distribute directions and materials to students. Go over project expectations and remind students that the art they create will act as a prompt for a persuasive writing piece.

3. Review the elements of persuasive writing as necessary, such as writing a phrase that becomes a call to action. Remind students to think about their purpose for writing. What are they trying to persuade others to do?

4. Next, write an environmentally conscious motto or slogan on the board, such as "Don't hug a tree, plant one!"

5. Begin a class discussion of why that may or may not be an effective motto.

6. Then, provide time for students to research important facts about recycling, conservation, reducing carbon emissions, and so on. They may be able to discover this information from science or social studies textbooks. Or have them conduct research online or in the library.

7. Invite students to come up with their own motto and create a poster to display it. Students should illustrate their poster to make it eye-catching and memorable, and then attach it to a stick.

8. Have students write a persuasive paragraph about their motto. An effective paragraph should include specific information that supports the motto and what students hope their motto will accomplish.

On or near Earth Day, silently march through school with signs. Once outside, chant a slogan, such as "Save Our Earth." If possible, march outside (but near) the school so your community can see, hear, and learn about Earth Day.

After the march, write ecological facts using chalk on the school's sidewalks. Remind students to use proper spelling and punctuation!

Earth Day, Hurrah!

Directions

1. Research important facts about recycling, conservation, reducing carbon emissions, and so on.

2. Come up with your own motto. Think about how your motto will persuade people to learn something new or act in a different way.

3. Create a poster to display your motto. Be sure to illustrate your poster to make it eye-catching and memorable, and then attach it to a stick.

4. Write a paragraph describing what you hope your motto will accomplish.

5. What did you learn from a classmate's motto? Think about how you might work together to accomplish your goals.

Materials

- posterboard
- colored markers
- stick
- tape
- sidewalk chalk

Choose one of the following ways to extend your learning:

Young Historian—Which neighborhood events have occurred to promote Earth Day since its founding in 1970?

Young Leader—Research ways in which your home, neighborhood, or town could be "greener." Write a persuasive letter (to a parent or politician) to share your ideas.

PROJECT CHECKLIST

☐ Poster is visually appealing and attracts attention.

☐ Motto generates reader interest.

☐ Paragraph persuades reader and explains the benefits of conservation, recycling, and so on.

☐ Check for correct spelling, grammar, punctuation, and capitalization.

Map Mania

Besides conveying information, maps can also be colorful works of art. Students will first study maps then create their own, incorporating (1) a compass rose, (2) latitude and longitude lines, (3) a legend or key, and (4) a scale.

Directions

1. Photocopy student directions and gather needed materials (see page 45).

2. Distribute directions and materials to students. Go over project expectations and let students know that the map they create will act as a prompt for a fictional story containing vivid descriptions.

3. Review the elements of descriptive writing, such as giving readers a strong sense of place, exciting events, and specific feelings.

4. Next, show students examples of maps that contain a compass rose (used for direction), legend or key, scale, and latitude/longitude lines. You can find a variety of imaginary maps online and project them in class. You may also find this site helpful in making classroom maps: www.press.uchicago.edu/books/akerman/maps_imaginary.html.

5. Invite students to draw their own map of an imaginary place with lots of color and detail. They may want to include map elements such as a compass rose, latitude and longitude lines, legend or key, and scale.

6. Encourage students to add interesting names for places on the map, such as The Valley of Friendship and Hillside of Hope.

7. Finally, have students write a short story that includes the physical world they mapped as the setting for the fictional story. Remind them to be as descriptive as possible.

Objectives

- Create a detailed visual map that provides a metaphorical setting for a descriptive story.

- Find examples of a literary device used in text and art.

- Create interesting place names or metaphors using human feelings.

Extra Dimension: Before students read their story to the class, photograph the maps and project them. Use the cursor to show where on the map the story is happening.

In the land of Kalite, the villagers believe in a myth. It tells of a rich prince traveling through the land to marry a daughter of a rich king. During his travels through Kalite, he was said to have been robbed. As he saw the robber sail away in the mist of Lost Lake, he heard a scream and saw the faint outline of another boat. It was much stranger than any he had seen before. When he tried to focus on the attackers, the mist thickened, and all he could see was a pair of thick green eyes staring back at him.

Excerpt from "Map Story" by Brian B., sixth grade

Map Mania

Directions

1. Draw a map of an imaginary place with lots of color and detail. Try sketching your map in pencil first and then add color.

2. You may want to include map elements such as a compass rose, latitude and longitude lines, a legend or key, and a scale.

3. Add interesting place names on the map. Try to create some that relate to human feelings, such as The Valley of Friendship and Hillside of Hope.

4. Write a short story up to 250 words that uses the place you mapped as a setting. Remember to be as descriptive as possible.

5. Trade papers with a partner to edit the story for style and consistency.

6. Be prepared to show your map and read your story in class.

Materials

- construction paper
- markers, crayons, or colored pencils
- ruler

Choose one of the following ways to extend your learning:

Young Historian—Identify which maps may have assisted European explorers in their travels. How do these maps differ from your imaginary map?

Young Mathematician—Use the scale on your map to determine how far one of your characters traveled during the story.

PROJECT CHECKLIST

- ☐ Map includes a variety of landforms and places.
- ☐ Story takes readers on a journey through your map.
- ☐ Precise adjectives and vivid verbs are used to suggest adventure.
- ☐ Check for correct spelling, grammar, punctuation, and capitalization.

The Room of My Dreams

Students draw and color their "dream room" in one-point perspective. Then, they write a short story that features action in the room they have created.

Directions

1. Photocopy student directions and gather needed materials (see page 47).

2. Distribute directions and materials to students. Go over project expectations and let students know that the art they create will act as a prompt for a fictional story containing vivid descriptions.

3. Review the elements of descriptive writing, such as using detail to show the reader setting, character, and feelings.

4. Next, introduce students to one-point perspective. You can find information about this online at www.olejarz.com/arted/perspective or at a similar Web site.

5. Provide time for students to practice one-point perspective using a pencil and ruler.

6. Invite students to draw their own "dream room." Encourage them to make it come alive with color and details. If desired, you may also provide glitter and glue.

7. Finally, have students write a short story that occurs in the dream room they have created. Remind them to be as descriptive as possible.

8. Allow time for students to share their artwork and story with the class.

Objectives

- Write multi-paragraph compositions.
- Use transition words within the composition.
- Proofread for correct English conventions.

Extra Dimension: Encourage students to choose a specific genre for their short story, such as mystery, romance, adventure, or thriller.

I stared around the room: the hideous orange and green striped couch against the west wall, the thick red carpet, the lavender walls, the French doors. They were everything I was leaving behind in this room. I wandered over to the sofa and sat down. I sunk down into it. After all the wear and tear it had been through, it was still the comfiest sofa I'd ever sat on. But it was hideous and more than 12 years old, so it was time to let it go.

"Emma," Charlie called to me. "Are you ready to leave, love?" Charlie stuck his head in the door and grinned at me. I stood up again and took one last breath in the room I was leaving.

"Yes, darling, I'm ready."

Excerpt from "The Room of My Dreams" by Mady S., eighth grade

The Room of My Dreams

Directions

1. Draw your "dream room" using one-point perspective. Using a ruler will help give your artwork a finished look.

2. Make your room come alive with color and details. Does your room have a theme? How do you feel when you imagine yourself in the room?

3. Write a short story up to 250 words that occurs in your dream room. Remember to be as descriptive as possible.

4. Include some dialogue in your story.

5. Trade papers with a partner to edit the story for style and consistency.

6. Be prepared to show your artwork and read your story in class.

Materials

- construction paper
- ruler
- pencil
- markers and crayons

Choose one of the following ways to extend your learning:

Young Designer—Using color and texture, devise an interior that reflects the mood and tone of the major character.

Young Linguist—Incorporate words and phrases from another language within the English story.

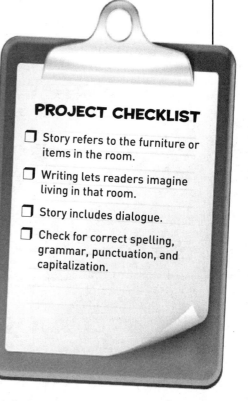

PROJECT CHECKLIST

- ☐ Story refers to the furniture or items in the room.
- ☐ Writing lets readers imagine living in that room.
- ☐ Story includes dialogue.
- ☐ Check for correct spelling, grammar, punctuation, and capitalization.

Pantoum Parade

A pantoum is an interesting poetic format in which the lines repeat in a prescribed pattern. Students can choose a topic or theme, then create artwork and a pantoum poem that support their idea.

Objectives

- Work through "writer's block" by focusing on a central theme.
- Explain the meaning of a complex word or idea.
- Rewrite and edit your work before publication.

Extra Dimension: Poetry is meant to be heard. Arrange a poetry reading, inviting another class or family members to come hear students' work.

Directions

1. Photocopy student directions and gather needed materials (see page 49).

2. Distribute directions and materials to students. Go over project expectations and let students know that the art they create will serve as the inspiration for a pantoum poem.

3. Review the history and elements of the pantoum form of poetry. (You can learn more about pantoums in Bonni Goldberg's book *Room to Write*.)

4. To begin, students should select a topic or theme, such as harmony, peace, friends, nature, laughter, love, faith, knowledge, achievement, growth, beauty, family, or something similar, that is important to them.

5. Have students use watercolors to create artwork that helps them visualize their topic or theme.

6. Then, students create an eight-line poem on their special topic. (Encourage them to write quickly and not to fuss over their ideas. Give them permission to change things later.) Students number the lines from 1 to 8 and arrange the eight lines into the following four-stanza sequence:
   - Stanza 1 consists of lines 1, 2, 3, 4.
   - Stanza 2 consists of lines 2, 5, 4, 6.
   - Stanza 3 consists of lines 5, 7, 6, 8.
   - Stanza 4 consists of lines 7, 1, 8, 3.

7. After students have written and finalized their pantoum, have them present it in a "four-pager" format. (See Step 6 on page 49.)

Almost Fall
by Alison H., eighth grade
The swishing of leaves in the wind through the fall's trees
The silent twitter of an invisible bird
The crunching of twigs beneath my feet
A running creek, water crashing against tiny pebbles at the bend

The silent twitter of an invisible bird
Sunlight turns green under the thick canopy
A running creek, water crashing against tiny pebbles at the bend
The far-off drumming from someone unseen

Sunlight turns green under the thick canopy
The sounds would be haunting if they weren't so beautiful
The far-off drumming from someone unseen
One single leaf, as yellow as the sun, falls at my feet

The sounds would be haunting if they weren't so beautiful
The swishing of leaves in the wind through the fall's trees
One single leaf, as yellow as the sun, falls at my feet
The crunching of twigs beneath my feet

Pantoum Parade

Directions

1. Choose a topic that is important to you. Consider harmony, peace, friends, nature, laughter, love, faith, knowledge, achievement, growth, beauty, or family.

2. Create artwork that helps you visualize your topic.

3. Next, write about your topic by creating eight lines quickly on your special topic. Use words, phrases, or complete sentences to express ideas—whatever comes to mind. You can always change things later.

4. When you are finished, number your lines from 1 to 8. Then, arrange your eight lines into the following four-stanza sequence:
   - Stanza 1 consists of lines 1, 2, 3, 4.
   - Stanza 2 consists of lines 2, 5, 4, 6.
   - Stanza 3 consists of lines 5, 7, 6, 8.
   - Stanza 4 consists of lines 7, 1, 8, 3.

5. Review your pantoum and revise as needed.

6. Create a four-pager out of construction paper:
   - Fold the paper in half.
   - Decorate the front and back covers.
   - Add the artwork that inspired your pantoum to page 2.
   - Include the pantoum itself on page 3.

7. Be prepared to show your artwork and read your pantoum in class.

Materials

- paper and pencil for writing and doodling
- watercolors and brushes
- construction paper

Choose one of the following ways to extend your learning:

Young Analyst—Use a pantoum to address a problem and solution.

Young Scientist—Write a pantoum about cell division.

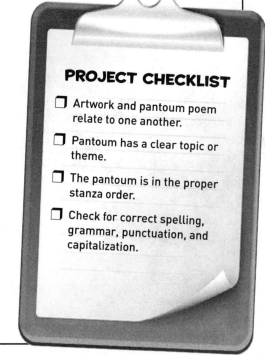

PROJECT CHECKLIST

- ☐ Artwork and pantoum poem relate to one another.
- ☐ Pantoum has a clear topic or theme.
- ☐ The pantoum is in the proper stanza order.
- ☐ Check for correct spelling, grammar, punctuation, and capitalization.

Magical Mandala

Mandalas have their origin in Eastern spirituality. They are geometric, colorful patterns that may sometimes represent the universe or aid in meditation. Students will create a mandala after they close their eyes and meditate on what is most important to them.

Objectives

- Listen and reflect attentively.
- Draw shapes and line, and experiment with color.
- Write from the heart.

Directions

1. Photocopy student directions and gather needed materials (see page 51).

2. Distribute directions and materials to students. Go over project expectations and let students know that the art they create will act as a prompt for a poem or paragraph containing vivid descriptions.

3. Review the elements of descriptive writing, such as featuring the senses, showing rather than telling the reader, and sharing human emotions.

4. Next, introduce the idea of mandalas by projecting some in the classroom or passing some around. Search online, or visit www.mandalarbre.com.

5. Play some quiet music and ask students to lower their heads on their desks as they close their eyes. Invite them to see shapes and colors, and to think about family, friends, spirit, and inner peace.

6. After a few minutes, or whenever the students are ready to begin, invite students to begin drawing a mandala.

7. Next, have students color their work.

8. Encourage students to let the artwork speak to them. Ask: *What is it saying to you?* They should put this message into words in their mandala-related descriptive poems or paragraphs.

by Mady S., eighth grade

Love is infinite . . .
Love is everywhere!
Hearts and thorns symbolize love.
Hearts show friendship.
Thorns signify pain.

Love is in need of a boundary line!
Let too much in and there'll be pain.
Love is like the shoreline.
It stretches itself out in vain!
      Excerpt from "What Is Love?"
      by Gendell F., eighth grade

Magical Mandala

Directions

1. Using the materials provided, begin drawing a mandala. Try adding both angular and circular forms.

2. Next, color your work.

3. Let the artwork speak to you. Ask yourself: *What is it saying to me?* Put this message into words in your mandala-related poem or paragraph.

4. Trade papers with a partner to edit the poem or paragraph for style and consistency.

5. Be prepared to show your mandala and read your poem or paragraph in class.

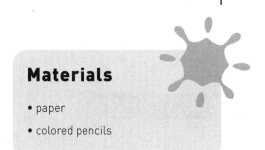

Materials

- paper
- colored pencils

Choose one of the following ways to extend your learning:

Young Sculptor—Create a 3-D image based on your mandala.

Young Mathematician—How is math a part of your mandala?

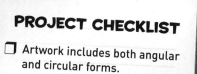

PROJECT CHECKLIST

- ☐ Artwork includes both angular and circular forms.
- ☐ Writing expresses feelings and desires to readers.
- ☐ Descriptive words are as exciting as the artwork.
- ☐ Check for correct spelling, grammar, punctuation, and capitalization.

Symmetry and Poetry

Students use paint to create a symmetrical design. They look at their creation and write a poem filled with figurative language about what they see. Students typically write fascinating poems, and they are thrilled to see the designs that appear before their eyes.

Objectives

- Write a poem with more than one poetic device.
- Translate visual imagery into written imagery.
- Craft a well-designed and neatly presented artistic and written work.

Extra Dimension: Invite students to share their poems with a partner. Have them discuss what they like about the other's poem. How are the poems similar and different? Point out simile, hyperbole, and rhyming couplets in the poems.

Directions

1. Photocopy student directions and gather needed materials (see page 53).

2. Distribute directions to students. Go over project expectations and let students know that the art they create will act as a prompt for a descriptive poem containing a simile, hyperbole, and two rhyming couplets.

3. Review the characteristics of the poetic literary devices.
   - A simile is a way of describing something by comparing it with something else. It uses the word *like* or *as* in the description.
   - Hyperbole is an exaggeration, used for effect, and not intended to be understood literally.
   - A rhyming couplet contains two lines that end with rhyming words.

4. Next, introduce the concept of symmetry and symmetrical design to students. If possible, show them examples of such artwork.

5. Then, give students paper and poster paint. Let them pour small droplets of poster paint colors onto their paper. Two or three different colors work well.

6. Tell students to fold their paper in half, press down on the sheet, and then open it to see a symmetrical design appear.

7. After giving them a few minutes to reflect on the design, have students write a poem about their artwork that contains (a) a simile, (b) hyperbole, and (c) two rhyming couplets.

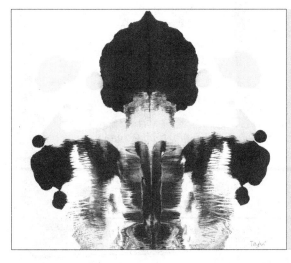

A Multicolored Person
by Taylor O., seventh grade
Splat! A multicolored person!
He stands like a superhero.
He saves a billion citizens.
The colors jump off the page.
His face is welcoming and kind.
He has a smart and crazy mind.
He shows his muscles and flies many miles,
And all of the way, his face shows big smiles.

Symmetry and Poetry

Directions

1. Pour small droplets of poster paint colors onto your paper. Two or three different colors work well.

2. Next, fold your paper in half, press down on the sheet. This will help spread the paint evenly across the folded paper.

3. Then, open it to see a symmetrical design appear.

3. Take a few minutes to reflect on the design.

4. Write a poem inspired by your art. Look for texture within the painted image that may inspire your poem. Describe what you see as your eyes move slowly across the artwork.

5. Include a simile, a hyperbole, and two rhyming couplets.

6. Trade papers with a partner to edit the poem for style and consistency.

7. Be prepared to show your artwork and read your poem in class.

Choose one of the following ways to extend your learning:

Young Dancer—Use shapes and images you see in your art to choreograph your own dance.

Young Scientist—Investigate the color spectrum. Which colors do you see in your artwork?

Materials

- poster paints
- construction paper

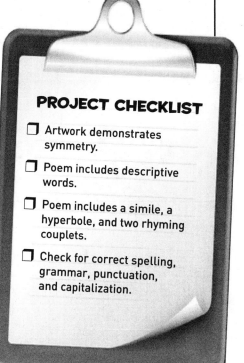

PROJECT CHECKLIST

☐ Artwork demonstrates symmetry.

☐ Poem includes descriptive words.

☐ Poem includes a simile, a hyperbole, and two rhyming couplets.

☐ Check for correct spelling, grammar, punctuation, and capitalization.

Yummy Adjectives

In this assignment, the art and writing go hand in hand. Adjectives add spice to writing. Students design their own restaurant menu, explain how the restaurant began, include yummy adjectives to describe the dishes on their menu, and feature a children's page of games and puzzles.

Objectives

- Read and comprehend unfamiliar words.
- Create a written piece for a specific audience using appropriate technology.
- Compare how text and art work together to express information.

Extra Dimension: Hold a potluck party. Invite students to bring in a dish from their "restaurant" to share with the class.

Directions

1. Photocopy student directions and gather needed materials (see page 55).

2. Distribute directions and materials to students. Go over project expectations and let students know that the menus they create should contain visuals and vivid descriptions using a variety of interesting adjectives.

3. Review the difference between dull, overused adjectives, and those that are more interesting and have more precise meanings.

4. Next, have students research pictures of culinary classics from a variety of cultures. Ask them which ethnic foods interest them and why.

5. Invite students to choose a theme for their restaurant.

6. Encourage them to investigate various menu categories (appetizers, main courses, desserts, children's menu, and so on).

7. Have students write a menu that includes adjectives to describe the culinary delights. Instruct them to add prices to make their menu more authentic.

8. Remind them to make the menu as informative and appetizing as possible. For example, students can

   - describe what any unusual "food words" mean.
   - list the color or texture of a dish.
   - use mouthwatering vocabulary.

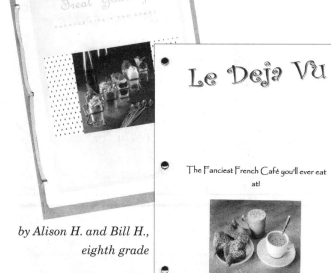

by Alison H. and Bill H., eighth grade

Le Deja Vu

The Fanciest French Café you'll ever eat at!

Soup du Jour—Bright Red Tomato Soup:
Every ounce is filled with lip-licking goodness.

Le Salad—Poached Chicken Salad:
Served on a bed of mixed greens, grilled vegetables, and pesto vinaigrette.

Magnificent and scrumptious!

*Excerpt from "Le Deja Vu" menu
by Francis T., eighth grade*

Yummy Adjectives

Directions

1. Choose a theme for your restaurant.

2. Investigate the various food categories that typically appear on a menu. Find out the meanings of any unusual culinary words.

3. Write a four-page menu that includes adjectives to describe the culinary delights. Descriptions of the dishes should include color or texture words.

4. Add prices and details about a chef or owner to make your menu more authentic.

5. You can write your menu by hand or use a computer and paste printouts to construction paper.

6. Be sure to add photos or illustrate your menu. Make your menu as colorful, decorative, informative, and appetizing as possible.

7. Trade papers with a partner to edit the menu for style and consistency.

8. Be prepared to show your artwork and read parts of your menu in class.

Materials

- construction paper
- crayons, colored pencils, and markers
- glue or tape

Choose one of the following ways to extend your learning:

Young Mathematician—A family of four has $75 to spend at your restaurant. What can they buy? Be certain to include appetizers and desserts among your choices! What amount will they tip the waiter?

Young Historian—Plan a menu for a specific culture, time, or event. For example, what would Thomas Jefferson have eaten in France during the eighteenth century?

Young Nutritionist—Plan a "heart-healthy" menu for your family.

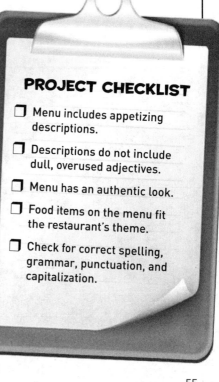

PROJECT CHECKLIST

- ❏ Menu includes appetizing descriptions.
- ❏ Descriptions do not include dull, overused adjectives.
- ❏ Menu has an authentic look.
- ❏ Food items on the menu fit the restaurant's theme.
- ❏ Check for correct spelling, grammar, punctuation, and capitalization.

Haiku Horizon

Writing a haiku can be a challenge, but the results are worth the effort. Students write a haiku based on a photo and present their work in a "four-pager" format with a decorated cover, a photo (or illustration), and a poem.

Directions

1. Photocopy student directions and gather needed materials (see page 57).

2. Distribute directions and materials to students. Go over project expectations and let students know that they will write a haiku poem based on a photo of their choice that depicts a nature scene.

3. Review the three-line haiku form of poetry. Nature is the subject matter and the poem occurs in the present tense. The first line has five syllables, the second line has seven syllables, and the third line has five.

4. Remind students that haiku poems present a perfect opportunity to be as descriptive as possible in just a few words.

5. Invite students to choose a picture they like online. They may also look for pictures in magazines, draw their own picture, or photograph a nature scene of their own.

6. Next, students write a three-line haiku as they look at their picture. Suggest that students write about how the picture affects them inside. Tell students to "write from the heart" or from their emotions, and to take a risk while writing.

7. Students make a four-pager that consists of a cover decorated as they like, the picture on page 2, and the haiku on page 3. Students may decorate the back cover or leave it blank.

Objectives

- Use figurative language.

- Write a haiku that is appropriate for your readers.

- Create a poem with emotional impact.

Extra Dimension: Read haikus to the class. Have students count out the 5-7-5 format.

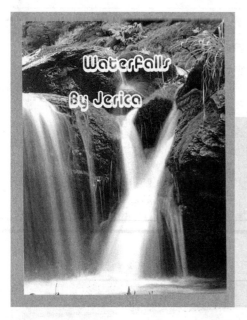

Jerica C., eighth grade, offers the emotional impact that she receives from a waterfall in this haiku.

Pretty waterfall
Calming me down so slightly
No whooshing away

Haiku Horizon

Directions

1. In a haiku, nature is the subject matter and the poem occurs in the present tense.
- The first line has five syllables.
- The second line has seven syllables.
- The third line has five.

Haiku poems present a perfect opportunity to be as descriptive as possible in just a few words.

2. Before writing your haiku, look for a nature photo online that you like. You may also look for pictures in magazines, draw your own picture, or take your own photograph of a nature scene.

3. Next, write a three-line haiku as you look at your picture. Is there anything unusual you notice in the image? Think about how the picture affects you inside. Write from the heart.

4. Once you've finished your poem, make a four-pager that consists of a cover decorated as you like, the picture on page 2, and the haiku on page 3. You may decorate the back cover or leave it blank. You may write your four-pager by hand or use a computer and paste printouts into the booklet.

5. Be prepared to show your artwork and read your haiku in class.

Choose one of the following ways to extend your learning:

Young Mathematician—Write a haiku to explain a concept such as fractions.

Young Historian—Write a haiku about a historical person you are studying.

Young Singer—Put your haiku to music! Write a "haiku song."

Materials
- construction paper
- glue
- colored pencils or markers

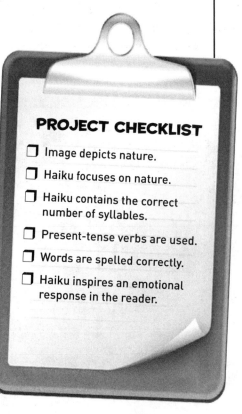

PROJECT CHECKLIST
- ☐ Image depicts nature.
- ☐ Haiku focuses on nature.
- ☐ Haiku contains the correct number of syllables.
- ☐ Present-tense verbs are used.
- ☐ Words are spelled correctly.
- ☐ Haiku inspires an emotional response in the reader.

Scene in Your Head

Often when teachers focus on reading comprehension, they may ask their students to visualize in their mind the scene they are reading. Ask students to draw the scene they see in their head. Once that image is fixed on paper, students may be more successful in writing what the scene means and how the characters react to each other.

Objectives

- Visualize and draw to enhance reading comprehension.
- Explain and justify an interpretation of text.
- Respond to fiction using interpretation and evaluation.

Directions

1. Photocopy student directions and gather needed materials (see page 59).

2. Distribute directions and materials to students. Go over project expectations and let students know that they will illustrate a scene from a book or play, just as they visualize it in their head. Remind them that the art they create will act as a prompt for a descriptive writing piece.

3. Review the purpose of descriptive writing, such as making a scene, character, or emotion come to life.

4. Next, direct students to read a chapter or a scene from a book or play.

5. Encourage them to focus on one event and draw it. Remind them to be as precise and colorful as possible to help make their descriptive piece more vivid.

6. Have students write a descriptive passage about the scene. Suggest that they focus on what the characters do and how they behave toward each other. How do they feel? How do the characters' feelings relate to students' own lives?

Extra Dimension: Make your own movie and bring an event or scene to life.

Cornelius: How am I going to get out of this? I am such an idiot for bringing Barnaby into all this. He is so young. He had a job, even though he works for Wolf Trap. Poor Barnaby. I have this nice, big wardrobe for hiding, but he has that extremely small work table. Oh, why does there have to be dust and perfume in this wardrobe? I hate allergies.

Barnaby: Oh! Why did I listen to Cornelius? I could have been home right now. I really hope Wolf Trap doesn't come over here and find me. What if I lose my job? What will mother do? Yikes! Oh, all this dust is really getting on my nose's nerves.

Excerpt from "The Matchmaker, Act 2: A Scene Description" *by Sairis P., sixth grade*

Scene in Your Head

Directions

1. First, read a chapter or a scene from a book or play.

2. As you read, focus on one event and how you visualize it.

3. Next, illustrate the scene. Imagine you are standing in the setting. What do you see, hear, smell, or feel? Remember to be as precise and colorful as possible, which will help make your descriptive writing piece more vivid.

Materials

- construction paper
- markers and crayons

4. Describe the scene in writing (about 250 words). Try to focus on what the characters do and how they behave toward each other. How do they feel? How do the characters' feelings relate to your own life?

5. Trade papers with a partner to edit the descriptive passage for style and consistency.

6. Be prepared to show your artwork and read your descriptive writing in class.

Choose one of the following ways to extend your learning:

Young Reader—Create a bibliography of additional books or plays this author has written.

Young Chef—Prepare a snack you believe characters in the book or play would eat.

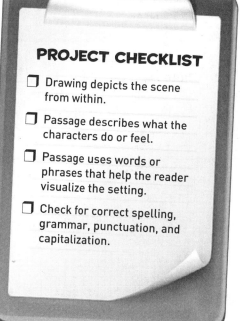

PROJECT CHECKLIST

☐ Drawing depicts the scene from within.

☐ Passage describes what the characters do or feel.

☐ Passage uses words or phrases that help the reader visualize the setting.

☐ Check for correct spelling, grammar, punctuation, and capitalization.

Narrative Writing Rubric

Telling Stories With a Beginning, Middle, and End

Simply put, narratives are (1) stories with attention-getting beginnings, (2) reversals and character discoveries in the middle, and (3) unexpected or satisfying endings. Many genres—myth, journal entries, mysteries, adventure stories, and more—are narratives.

	1 Novice	2 Discoverer	3 Achiever	4 Hero
Ideas and Organization	Lacks purpose, main idea, details, and sequence (beginning, middle, end).	Unclear main idea, details, and sequence.	Clearly stated main idea, details, and sequence.	Thoroughly explained main idea, details, and sequence.
Word Choice	Excessive incorrect use of words, and repetitive, limited vocabulary.	Generally correct words; some variation in language, and attempts to interest the reader.	Interesting use of effective verbs and specific vocabulary to interest readers.	Compelling vocabulary, creative variety, and dynamic use of figurative language to allure readers.
Structure, Grammar, and Mechanics	Lacks evidence of proper use of complete sentences, proper spelling, punctuation, or grammar.	Exhibits some understanding of sentence structure; many spelling, punctuation, and grammatical errors.	Shows sentence variety, with few errors in spelling, punctuation, or grammar.	Offers readers engaging and compelling sentences and paragraphs without spelling, punctuation, or grammatical errors.
Creative Presentation and Art	Lacks originality and neatness; is generally illegible.	Attempts to exhibit care in originality, neatness.	Offers an original concept and a focused, neat presentation.	Presents a novel concept rendered in an impeccable and pleasing presentation.

Notes _____

_____

_____

Key
14–16 points: Excellent
11–13 points: Very Good
8–10 points: Good
5–7 points: Fair
0–4 points: Poor

Score

Awesome Art Projects That Spark Super Writing • Copyright © 2011 by Jan Wiezorek, Scholastic Teaching Resources

Expository Writing Rubric

Fact-Telling About People, Places, and Ideas

Expository writing plays an important role in such fields as journalism, science, social studies, art history, and many other disciplines. Providing facts and explaining what they mean are at the heart of expository writing. Web pages, text messages, television newscasts, brochures, newspaper accounts, research papers, and documentaries are examples of expository writing.

Answering the five Ws and H—who, what, when, where, why, and how—is what expository writing is all about.

	1 Novice	2 Discoverer	3 Achiever	4 Hero
Ideas and Organization	Lacks 5 Ws, H; no evidence of organized, logical thought.	Exhibits some of the 5 Ws, H; attempts to present ideas in an orderly way.	Clearly presents the 5 Ws, H; takes the reader through a logical sequence of ideas.	Provides compelling 5 Ws, H; explains why the reader should care about this information in a logical way; offers additional research.
Word Choice	Uses incorrect words to express ideas; no use of appropriate academic language or vocabulary central to the discussion.	Generally correct words; some variation in language or use of academic words and vocabulary necessary to explain the concept.	Thorough understanding of the concept leads writer to use academic language and comparisons that make the concept interesting to the reader.	Exciting retelling of the facts using academic language, compare-contrast analysis, and figurative language.
Structure, Grammar, and Mechanics	Lacks evidence of proper use of complete sentences, proper spelling, punctuation, or grammar.	Exhibits some understanding of sentence structure; many spelling, punctuation, and grammatical errors.	Shows sentence variety, with few errors in spelling, punctuation, or grammar.	Offers readers engaging and compelling sentences and paragraphs without spelling, punctuation, or grammatical errors.
Creative Presentation and Art	No concern for neatness, balance, or creative use of materials; nearly illegible.	Attempts to show careful work that is neat and balanced; somewhat easy to read.	Features originality, neatness, creative use of materials; reader-friendly.	Provides a colorful work that exhibits original thought and careful construction; attention-getting.

Notes _____

_____

_____

Key
14–16 points: Excellent
11–13 points: Very Good
8–10 points: Good
5–7 points: Fair
0–4 points: Poor

Score

Persuasive Writing Rubric

Presenting Arguments and Counterarguments

Telling your point of view and defending it in writing are important skills to have. In persuasive writing, the writer gives arguments and explains his or her point of view. Persuasive writing will usually debunk alternative viewpoints by providing a counterargument. It states why other views are less than ideal.

	1 Novice	2 Discoverer	3 Achiever	4 Hero
Ideas and Organization	No evidence of an argument or counterargument; lacks logic.	Some attempt to present a logical and specific point of view.	Offers a well-developed argument and counterargument.	Provides a detailed argument, counterargument, and supporting research.
Word Choice	Provides no language or vocabulary appropriate to the discussion.	Uses some terminology related to the argument.	Uses persuasive words and terminology to sway the reader.	Uses language to provide a persuasive case for a specific viewpoint; language also works to debunk alternative views.
Structure, Grammar, and Mechanics	Lacks evidence of proper use of complete sentences, proper spelling, punctuation, or grammar.	Exhibits some understanding of sentence structure; many spelling, punctuation, and grammatical errors.	Shows sentence variety, with few errors in spelling, punctuation, or grammar.	Offers readers engaging and compelling sentences and paragraphs without spelling, punctuation, or grammatical errors.
Creative Presentation and Art	No evidence of design sense to persuade the reader.	Some care to present a persuasive point of view through art.	Offers persuasive design, color, balance, and imagery.	Effectively uses art concepts and emotional appeal to sway the reader toward a specific viewpoint.

Notes _____

_____

_____

Key
14–16 points: Excellent
11–13 points: Very Good
 8–10 points: Good
 5–7 points: Fair
 0–4 points: Poor

Score

Descriptive Writing Rubric

Using Sensory Images, Precise Adjectives, and Vivid Verbs

Readers enjoy descriptive writing because it helps them see someone or something in a new way. Using words and images that bring sight, smell, touch, taste, and hearing to life are crucial to good descriptive writing. Powerful adjectives can help tell a descriptive story, too.

	1 Novice	2 Discoverer	3 Achiever	4 Hero
Ideas and Organization	No evidence of a purpose or logical ideas that help the reader see what is being described.	Hints at using organized ideas to describe people, places, and things.	Well-focused sentences and paragraphs are logical and help readers see what is being described.	Interesting and precise sentences and paragraphs tell a descriptive story with metaphor.
Word Choice	Lacks evidence of sensory words and adjectives.	Provides some sensory words and adjectives.	Uses well-crafted sensory images and appropriate adjectives that describe.	Engages the reader in the story by making people, places, and objects come alive with sensory details, comparisons, and powerful adjectives.
Structure, Grammar, and Mechanics	Lacks evidence of proper use of complete sentences, proper spelling, punctuation, or grammar.	Exhibits some understanding of sentence structure; many spelling, punctuation, and grammatical errors.	Shows sentence variety, with few errors in spelling, punctuation, or grammar.	Offers readers engaging and compelling sentences and paragraphs without spelling, punctuation, or grammatical errors.
Creative Presentation and Art	No sense of artistic concern or care for neatness; no attempt to interest the reader through sensory detail.	Provides some concern for artistic technique and neatness; offers basic description.	Exhibits strong use and understanding of artistic concepts; details figure strongly in the work.	Creative use of materials to tell an engaging story artistically; powerful details and description.

Notes _____

_____

_____

Key
14–16 points: Excellent
11–13 points: Very Good
8–10 points: Good
5–7 points: Fair
0–4 points: Poor

Score

Web Resources and Bibliography

Web Resources to Investigate

www.artandwriting.org (Scholastic's recognition program for creative students in grades 7–12)

www.ectolearning.com (Valuable learning site for teachers and students)

www.eduscapes.com/tap/topic92.htm (Electronic postcards)

www.makebeliefscomix.com (Make your own comics)

www.poeticpower.com (Poetry online contest submissions)

www.readwritethink.org (Lesson plans and materials for students)

www.studentreasures.com (Book publishing program)

www.teenink.com (Teen stories and online submissions)

www.wikipedia.com (Research Web site)

www2.actden.com/writ_den/tips/contents.htm (Paragraph-writing tips)

Bibliography

Baer, Allison L. "Creating a Shared Definition of Good and Bad Writing Through Revision Strategies," *Middle School Journal*, March 2008, 46–53.

Barton, Jim et al. "They Want to Learn How to Think: Using Art to Enhance Comprehension," *Language Arts, 85, (2)*, November 2007, 125–133.

Beckett, Sister Wendy. *Sister Wendy's 1000 Masterpieces*. New York: DK Publishing, 1999.

Beckett, Sister Wendy. *Sister Wendy's Story of Painting*. New York: DK Publishing, 1994.

Callihan, E. L. *Grammar for Journalists*. Radnor, PA: Chilton, 1969.

Cornett, Claudia A. "Center Stage. Arts-Based Read-Alouds," *The Reading Teacher*, 60, (3), November 2006, 234–240.

Cortines, R. *Gaining the Arts Advantage*. Washington: President's Committee on the Arts and Humanities, 1999.

Edwards, Betty. *The New Drawing on the Right Side of the Brain*. New York: Penguin Putnam, 1999.

Exercises in English. Chicago: Loyola Press, 2008.

Gardner, Howard. *Frames of Mind*. New York: Basic, 1983.

Goldberg, Bonni. *Room to Write*. New York: Penguin Putnam, 1996.

Hume, Helen D. *A Survival Kit for the Elementary/Middle School Art Teacher*. San Francisco: Jossey-Bass, 2000.

Killgallon, Don and Jenny Killgallon. *Grammar for Middle School: A Sentence-Composing Approach*. Portsmouth, NH: Heinemann, 2006.

Martin, David F. and Lee A. Jacobus. *Humanities Through the Arts*. New York: Penguin Putnam, 2004.

Marzano, Robert et al. *Classroom Instruction That Works: Research-Based Strategies for Increasing Student Achievement*. Alexandria, VA: Association for Supervision and Curriculum Development, 2001.

May, Rollo. *Courage to Create*. New York: Norton, 1994.

Meyer, Herbert E. and Jill M. Meyer. *How to Write*. Washington: Storm King Press, 2003.

Nelms, Henning. *Thinking With a Pencil*. New York: HarperCollins, 1964.

Watson, Ernest and Aldren Watson. *Watson Drawing Book*. New York: Bell, 1962.